WHY DOES MY BODY DO THAT?

COUGH

by Rachel Rose

Consultant: Beth Gambro
Reading Specialist, Yorkville, Illinois

Minneapolis, Minnesota

Teaching Tips

Before Reading

- Look at the cover of the book. Discuss the picture and the title.
- Ask readers to brainstorm a list of what they already know about coughs. What can they expect to see in this book?
- Go on a picture walk, looking through the pictures to discuss vocabulary and make predictions about the text.

During Reading

- Read for purpose. Encourage readers to think about coughs as they are reading.
- Ask readers to look for the details of the book. What are they learning about the body and how it coughs?
- If readers encounter an unknown word, ask them to look at the sounds in the word. Then, ask them to look at the rest of the page. Are there any clues to help them understand?

After Reading

- Encourage readers to pick a buddy and reread the book together.
- Ask readers to name two things that can cause coughs. Find the pages that tell about these things.
- Ask readers to write or draw something they learned about coughs.

Credits: Cover and title page, © Jason Finn/Shutterstock and © farzand01/Shutterstock; 3, © AaronAmat/iStock; 5, © SDI Productions/iStock; 7, © lechatnoir/iStock and © Poltu shyamal/iStock; 8–9, © Jolanta Mosakovska/Shutterstock; 11, © Pixel-Shot/Shutterstock; 13, © KatarzynaBialasiewicz/iStock and © tylim/iStock; 14–15, © dima_sidelnikov/iStock; 17, © Riska/iStock; 18, © subjug/iStock; 18–19, © Prostock-Studio/iStock; 21, © ti-ja/iStock; 22, © Tetiana Lazunova/iStock; 23TL, © Zuberka/iStock; 23TC, © SDI Productions/iStock; 23TR, © fatido/iStock; 23BL, © magicmine/iStock; 23BC, © Harbucks/iStock; and 23BR, © sankalpmaya/iStock.

Library of Congress Cataloging-in-Publication Data

Names: Rose, Rachel, 1968- author.
Title: Cough / by Rachel Rose.
Description: Bearcub books. | Minneapolis, Minnesota : Bearport Publishing
  Company, [2023] | Series: Why does my body do that? | Includes
  bibliographical references and index.
Identifiers: LCCN 2022023112 (print) | LCCN 2022023113 (ebook) | ISBN
  9798885093361 (library binding) | ISBN 9798885094580 (paperback) | ISBN
  9798885095730 (ebook)
Subjects: LCSH: Cough--Juvenile literature. | Reflexes--Juvenile
  literature.
Classification: LCC QP123.5 .R67 2023 (print) | LCC QP123.5 (ebook) | DDC
  612.2--dc23/eng/20220517
LC record available at https://lccn.loc.gov/2022023112
LC ebook record available at https://lccn.loc.gov/2022023113

Copyright © 2023 Bearport Publishing Company. All rights reserved. No part of this publication may be reproduced in whole or in part, stored in any retrieval system, or transmitted in any form or by any means, electronic, mechanical, photocopying, recording, or otherwise, without written permission from the publisher.

For more information, write to Bearport Publishing, 5357 Penn Avenue South, Minneapolis, MN 55419.

Contents

A Loud Sound 4

See It Happen 22

Glossary 23

Index 24

Read More 24

Learn More Online 24

About the Author 24

A Loud Sound

My **throat** feels dry and scratchy.

Suddenly, I make a loud sound.

Cough!

Why does my body do that?

Everyone coughs.

You may cough many times in a row.

Other times, your cough may be short and quick.

How do coughs happen?

Sometimes, you **breathe** in things that are bad for your body.

Your brain tells your body to get rid of them.

Your chest and belly **squeeze**.

This pushes air out of your **lungs**.

Part of your throat opens to let the air out.

It makes the cough sound.

Sometimes, people cough when they breathe in dust.

People also cough if something gets stuck in their throat.

Some **germs** can make you cough, too.

This may happen when you are sick with a cold or the **flu**.

When you cough, the germs leave your body.

Remember to cover your mouth!

This keeps the germs away from other people.

What can make you cough less?

Sipping a warm drink helps.

You could suck on a cough drop, too.

A cough may bother you.

But it is usually good for your body.

It means your body is working hard to stay healthy.

See It Happen

You breathe in tiny things that are not good for you.

Your brain tells your belly and chest to squeeze.

This pushes air into your throat and out of your mouth.

Glossary

breathe to take air in and let it out of the body

flu a kind of sickness

germs tiny things that can make people sick

lungs parts of the body that help you breathe

squeeze to press tightly

throat the tube inside the neck

Index

belly 10, 22
brain 8, 22
breathe 8, 12, 22
chest 10, 22
germs 14, 16
lungs 10
mouth 16, 22
throat 4, 10, 12, 22

Read More

Throp, Claire. *Read All about the Human Body (Read All about It!).* North Mankato, MN: Pebble Sprout, 2021.

Wendt, Jennifer. *My Lungs (What's Inside Me?).* Minneapolis: Bearport Publishing, 2022.

Learn More Online

1. Go to **www.factsurfer.com** or scan the QR code below.
2. Enter "**Cough**" into the search box.
3. Click on the cover of this book to see a list of websites.

About the Author

Rachel Rose lives in California. When she is sick with a cough, she loves to stay in bed and read a good book!